Frederick Dougla...

A Slave Biography

Contents

Written by Amanda Mitchison

Illustrated by Lee Sullivan

Early childhood

Frederick Douglass was born
as Frederick Bailey in 1817
on a farm in Maryland, in
the United States of America.
His mother was a slave and soon
after he was born, she was sent
to a farm 12 miles away to work
and Frederick was brought
up by his grandmother,
Betsey Bailey.

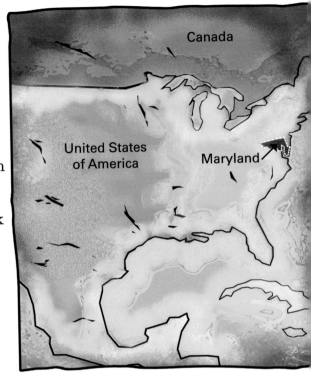

Canada

United States
of America

Maryland

Frederick never knew his parents. It was clear from his features that his father had been a white man, and some whispered that his master, Captain Aaron Anthony, was his father, but Frederick could never be sure of this.

His mother, who was also owned by Captain Anthony, didn't visit often. It was a long walk home for her and she would arrive late at night and be gone again by morning. Later Frederick wrote that he did not remember ever seeing her by the light of day, and when he was about seven, she died.

Conditions of slaves

In the early 19th century, when Frederick was growing up, slavery was illegal in most of the northern states of America. But in the southern states it was a different matter. One in three Americans living in the South was a slave. These slaves were nearly all black people. They themselves, or their parents, or their grandparents, or their great-grandparents, had been captured and brought over in ships from Africa.

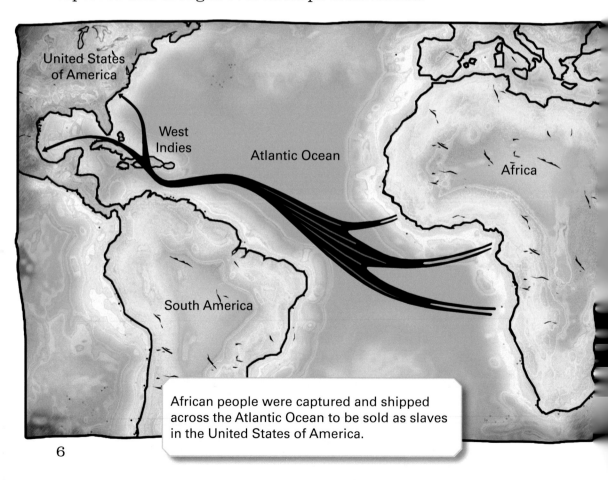

African people were captured and shipped across the Atlantic Ocean to be sold as slaves in the United States of America.

Some slaves were house servants, but most were farm **labourers**.
Conditions were harsh, especially on the big farms
called "plantations". Many plantation slaves were starving
and lived in tiny shacks that were freezing in winter and bred
disease in the hot summers.

slaves picking cotton on a plantation

7

Children whose parents were slaves
were soon put to work. At five years
old they'd start to run errands such
as carrying water. By the age
of 12 they'd be out working
in the fields from daybreak
until sundown,
and often longer if
there was a
full moon.

Slaves had no rights. Their masters could whip them, or starve
them, or even kill them. They could expect to be sold at least
once in their lifetime and to be separated from their families
and loved ones.

At auctions they were prodded and made to jump and dance. Their teeth were examined as if they were horses and they were often stripped to show how strong they were and how little whipping they needed.

Not all African Americans in the South were slaves. There were also "free blacks" who'd been granted their freedom by their owners or had managed to buy their freedom. But free blacks did not have the same rights as white citizens, and were only allowed to do certain jobs. There were different laws for black people, too. They had to use separate public toilets. Trains and boats and buses had "whites only" and "**negro**" carriages and compartments.

a painting of a slave auction in Richmond, Virginia in 1861

9

Plantation life

When Frederick was 7 or 8, he was thought to be old enough to start working. So he left his grandmother's cabin and went to live in Captain Anthony's house in the middle of the plantation.

Captain Anthony worked for Colonel Lloyd, who owned the plantation. He had a huge house, over 1,000 slaves and a wonderful garden growing every type of fruit tree: apples, oranges, peaches, apricots and cherries. Lloyd had great difficulty keeping his hungry slaves from eating his fruit and, in the end, he had the fence around his orchard covered in sticky black tar. Any slave found with tar marks on his clothes or skin was whipped for having tried to climb into the orchard. Slaves were whipped for any type of **disobedience** and Frederick never forgot seeing his aunt Hester viciously beaten for secretly meeting up with a young man who she loved.

Frederick was careful to stay out of trouble.
His job was to sweep the yard and drive
the cows home in the evening.
All he had to wear was a long shirt
down to his knees. At mealtimes a big
wooden plate of cornmeal mush
was put down and all the children
gathered round and scooped
it up with bits of wood or
oyster shells. But there was
never enough.

Sometimes Frederick was so hungry that he would follow
the servant girl outside when she was shaking out the master's
tablecloth and he would scrabble with the cats for crumbs and
chicken bones. At night he slept on the kitchen floor. To keep
warm in the winter he stole a corn sack to wrap around himself,
but his feet still cracked from the cold.

Frederick's first trousers

When Frederick was about 10 years old, he was told that he was leaving the plantation, to go to Baltimore, 100 miles away, to work for Sophia and Hugh Auld. The Aulds were relatives of Captain Anthony's and they wanted Frederick to come and look after their young son, Thomas.

Frederick was very excited at the idea of going to a city, and even more excited that in order to be a city slave, he'd need a pair of trousers – his first pair of trousers! Before he got them, he had to be clean and scrub all the dirt off his knees and feet. Frederick was so eager that he scrubbed himself until he was sore. But he didn't mind – he was delighted with his new trousers.

On a Saturday morning Frederick sailed down the river to Baltimore sitting in the bows of a sailing boat filled with sheep. He gave one last glance to Colonel Lloyd's plantation and never looked back.

Learning to read and write

Frederick loved Baltimore. City slaves, he soon discovered, were better fed and treated than the slaves on the plantations. They also didn't work such long hours and had time to learn new skills. Some female slaves became dressmakers and the men often picked up ship-building trades. This meant they could earn a little money for themselves.

Baltimore in 1836

Frederick's mistress Sophia Auld was kind to him and started teaching him to read. He was a quick learner, but Hugh Auld put a stop to the lessons, because he thought that if Frederick learnt to read he'd find out too much about the world and would no longer accept being owned and controlled by someone else.

But it was too late – Frederick had caught the reading bug. Now he studied in secret, sneaking out of the house with a book and some bread from the kitchen. In the street he'd meet up with the poor local white boys. In exchange for bread, they helped him with his reading.

He started to write, copying out words with lumps of chalk on pavements and brick walls. Later, he managed to steal old exercise books that young Thomas Auld had used in school. Frederick filled in the gaps between the lines, mimicking the boy's handwriting.

By the time he was 13, Frederick could read and write and his handwriting was good (and rather similar to Thomas Auld's!).

From that point on, he read whatever he could. With 50 cents that he was given for running errands, he bought a book of political speeches and essays. He read the book over and over again and became certain that slavery was wrong.

Frederick knew that slavery would continue as long as slaves were kept uneducated, so he started teaching a group of young black people to read and write. Also, in Baltimore, he could keep up with the thriving **abolitionist** movement, which was trying to stop slavery.

Covey the slave-breaker

The more Frederick read, the more he hated slavery. To his slave-owners, he was no longer the cheerful, eager-to-please boy he'd been before. Hugh Auld was right – literacy had made it difficult for Frederick to accept his life as a slave.

When he was 15 he was sent to live with Hugh Auld's brother Thomas in a nearby small town. Thomas Auld didn't like Frederick's attitude and hired him out for a year to Edward Covey, a poor local farmer with a reputation as a "slave-breaker". A slave-breaker was someone who could "break" the **spirit** and will of difficult slaves, usually by beating them very violently and very often.

On Covey's farm Frederick worked morning, noon and night. Work, work, work. If Frederick ever stopped, Covey was on to him immediately. The slaves nicknamed Covey "the snake" because he'd sneak up on them. When they were out in the fields he'd crawl towards them through the high corn and suddenly pop up by their side shouting, "Ha, ha! Dash on, dash on!" And, if they didn't dash, they were beaten.

Frederick was always being beaten and soon he did begin to feel "broken". He was utterly worn out, too tired to read or even to think. Sundays were his only time off and he'd spend the day exhausted under a tree.

After one particularly brutal beating, Frederick escaped. He arrived at Thomas Auld's house covered in blood. But, despite Frederick's pleas, Thomas Auld sent him back saying that Covey "owned" him for a year.

Frederick returned to Covey but he'd had enough of the beatings. And when Covey approached him with a rope to tie him up for a whipping, Frederick wrestled his master to the ground.

Afterwards Frederick assumed he'd be put in prison and probably hanged – because slaves could be **executed** for standing up to their masters. But Covey never beat him again. Later Frederick wrote about how standing up to Covey made him feel strong: "I gained the self-confidence and determination to be a free man."

Failed escape

In January 1835, when Frederick was about 17, he was hired out to another, kinder farmer. Here he was given enough food to eat and enough time to eat it. He also worked shorter hours and he used his time off to set up a secret Sunday school in the woods where he taught slaves to read and write. Soon he was holding evening classes as well.

But despite his living conditions being better, Frederick was still determined to control his own life and be free. So after a year with his new master, he decided to run away.

He and five other men hatched a plan to steal a large canoe and paddle 70 miles out of Chesapeake Bay towards the Delaware River and up into Pennsylvania, which was a free state where slavery was illegal. In case they were stopped, each man carried a letter of free passage from his owner – the letters were **forged** by Frederick.

The plan was very dangerous – the water in the bay could be as rough as open sea and the men would have to find their way by following the North Star. In the end they never even set off. Someone betrayed them and they were rounded up, roped to the back of horses and dragged off to jail.

Back in Baltimore

Frederick stayed in prison for a week.
The other men were quickly returned
to their old masters, but because
Frederick was the ring-leader,
the local slave-owners wanted
to get rid of him. So Thomas Auld
sent him back to stay with his
brother Hugh in Baltimore.

Frederick was now a tall,
strong young man and Hugh
Auld hired out him out to local
ship-building yards. Frederick
learnt to become a caulker –
making ships watertight by
sealing up the seams and joints
between the planks of wood with
a mixture of tar and rope.
Frederick was good at his job and
worked hard. He wasn't whipped
any more, but he certainly
wasn't free. He had to give his
earnings to Hugh Auld.

Now Frederick had plenty of spare time. He learnt to play the violin and joined a local debating club for black people. Here he had his first experiences of speaking at public meetings and met Anna Murray, an African American woman with whom he became great friends.

Anna Murray

Escape to New York

Anna Murray, unlike Frederick, was a free black. Her parents had been slaves who'd bought their freedom from their owners just a month before she was born. She had never learnt to read and write, but she was very careful with

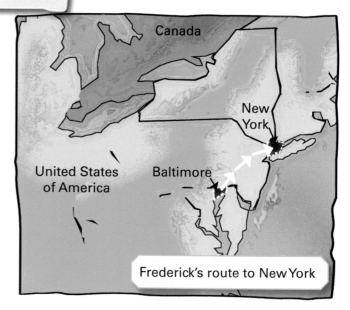

Frederick's route to New York

money and had savings, so it was thanks to her and a loan she gave him for his travel that Frederick finally managed to make his escape to New York.

For the journey Frederick borrowed a sailor's identity papers from a free black man and then, dressed like a sailor, he boarded a train north. He was nervous because the sailor's papers didn't match his own appearance at all. But the ticket conductor never bothered to check.

Afterwards Frederick caught a steam boat, and then took a second train that brought him to New York City. At last, he was free!

New York

But even in New York, Frederick was not safe. Southern slave-catchers roamed the streets, and the walls of buildings were pasted with "Wanted" posters with drawings and descriptions of runaway slaves. There were big rewards offered for their capture and Frederick knew he wasn't safe.

$150 REWARD

RANAWAY from the subscriber, on the night of the 2d instant, a negro man, who calls himself *Henry May*, about 22 years old, 5 feet 6 or 8 inches high, ordinary color, rather chunky built, bushy head, and has it divided mostly on one side, and keeps it very nicely combed; has been raised in the house, and is a first rate dining-room servant, and was in a tavern in Louisville for 18 months. I expect he is now in Louisville trying to make his escape to a free state, (in all probability to Cincinnati, Ohio.) Perhaps he may try to get employment on a steamboat. He is a good cook, and is handy in any capacity as a house servant. Had on when he left, a dark cassinett coatee, and dark striped cassinett pantaloons, new—he had other clothing. I will give $50 reward if taken in Louisville; 100 dollars if taken one hundred miles from Louisville in this State, and 150 dollars if taken out of this State, and delivered to me, or secured in any jail so that I can get him again.

Bardstown, Ky., September 3d, 1838.   **WILLIAM BURKE.**

a poster offering a reward for a runaway slave

Frederick didn't know anyone in the city, but he did have the address of David Ruggles, a black man who was part of the "Underground Railroad". This was a chain of "stations" or secret safe houses and hideaways for runaway slaves that went from the South all the way to Canada, where slaves could be free and safe from slave-catchers.

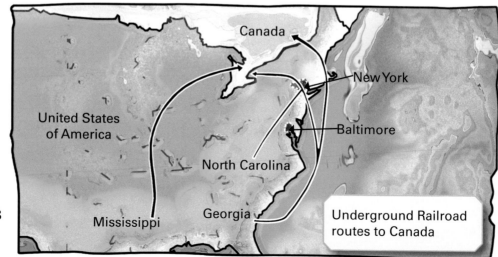

Canada

New York

United States of America

Baltimore

North Carolina

Georgia

Mississippi

Underground Railroad routes to Canada

On the railroad, the "passengers" were the runaway slaves and the "station masters" were the brave people, like Ruggles, who took them in. During the 19th century, tens of thousands of black Americans used the railroad to escape to freedom.

Ruggles took Frederick in and, from his house, Frederick sent a letter to Anna asking her to join him. When she arrived in New York, they got married. To put the slave-catchers off his scent, Frederick signed the marriage certificate as "Frederick Johnson". Later he discovered that there were many slaves called Johnson, so he changed his name a second time to "Douglass".

New Bedford

Ruggles advised the young couple to move to New Bedford in Massachusetts. New Bedford was a port where Frederick could look for work as a ships' caulker. The town was also a centre for the abolitionist movement, where slave-catchers were not welcome, so it was safer than New York.

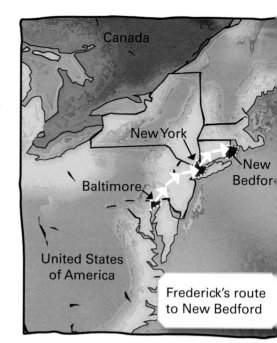

Frederick's route to New Bedford

a ship being repaired in New Bedford harbour in the 19th century

Frederick liked New Bedford, but even here there was
still plenty of **prejudice** against black people.
The churches had separate areas for black
people to sit in and some public halls
were closed to them. In the shipyards,
white men refused to work alongside
black men. This meant Frederick
could not get work as a caulker.
Instead he had to take any
poorly paid labouring job
he could find. He shovelled
coal and dug cellars
and helped load
and unload ships.

Frederick becomes a public speaker

In New Bedford someone gave Frederick a copy of *The Liberator*. This was the newspaper of the American Anti-Slavery Society, which was campaigning for the freeing of all slaves in the United States. Frederick was very

excited by what he read and he kept a copy of the newspaper on his bedside table beside his Bible.

Soon Frederick was a regular at anti-slavery meetings. In 1841, he gave his first speech for the society. It was a great success – he was a **fluent** and confident speaker. He recounted his life and his escape from slavery and gave gruesome details about how slaves were beaten and starved.

Frederick also made his audience laugh. He gave a very funny account of overcoming the slave-breaker, Covey, and did imitations of people who were pro-slavery. Afterwards the editor of *The Liberator*, William Lloyd Garrison, gave Frederick a job travelling the country giving anti-slavery talks and selling his newspaper.

On the road

It wasn't easy being on the road. Frederick now had a young
family and he had to leave Anna and the children behind for weeks
on end as he travelled across the United States. Often he stayed
in miserable lodging houses and, because he refused to travel in
"negro" carriages, he was forever being pulled out of "whites only"
seats by ticket collectors and porters.

Sometimes even the meetings were violent. In the town of Pendleton in Indiana, Frederick was set upon by pro-slavery thugs who broke his hand.

But the more Frederick spoke, the better his talks became and he widened his argument to talk not only about slavery but also about the poor treatment of black people in the North. In fact, he soon became too good at speaking. Some of his listeners began to doubt that he'd ever been a slave. They thought it was impossible that someone who'd never been to school could argue so well and sound so educated.

the police hold back the crowds while Frederick speaks in Boston

Trip to Britain

To prove he really had been a slave, Frederick wrote a book about his life, and included the names of his owners and the places where he'd lived. *The Narrative of the Life of Frederick Douglass, an American Slave, Written By Himself*, came out in 1845 and was an instant bestseller.

But publishing his autobiography was a huge risk – Frederick was still an escaped slave and legally the property of the Aulds. At any time a slave-catcher could seize him and return him to his owners.

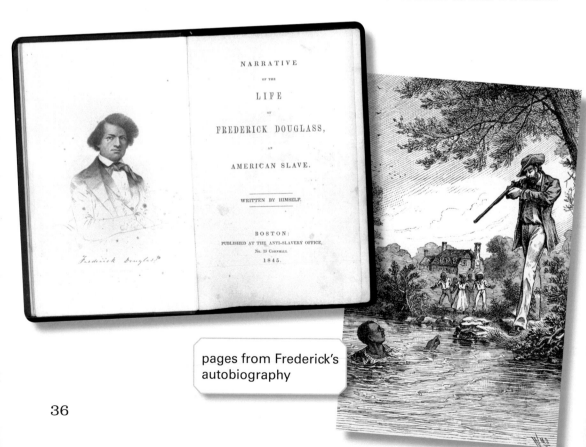

pages from Frederick's autobiography

Frederick knew he'd be safer abroad, so a tour of Britain
and Ireland giving talks was quickly planned for him
and he boarded a ship for Liverpool. He left Anna and his four
children behind.

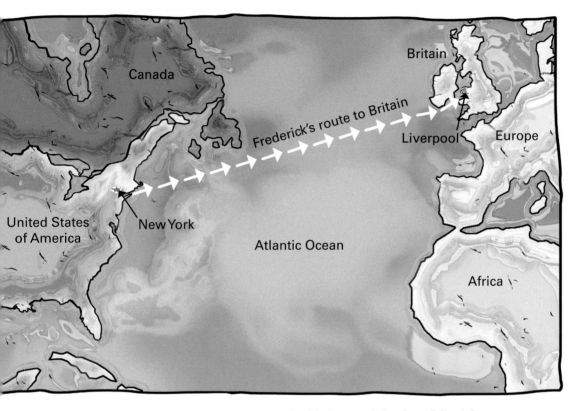

Frederick spent two years touring Britain and Ireland but he
missed his family and wanted to return home. Some English
friends solved the problem – they raised £150 and bought his
freedom from the Aulds.

Frederick was now able to return to the United States as a free man.

Frederick sets up a newspaper

When Frederick came home he started up his own newspaper, *The North Star*. It soon became the best-known black newspaper in the United States.

slaves fleeing on the Underground Railroad

Frederick at the time of the first edition of *The North Star* in 1847

Frederick was now probably the most famous and influential black man in the United States and he and Anna became very active in the Underground Railroad, helping slaves to escape.

The family had now moved to
Rochester near to the Canadian
border and sometimes Frederick
would go to work in the morning
and find runaway slaves sitting on
the steps of his office. At times he
and Anna had 10 or more runaway
slaves staying in their house at once.

The American Civil War

By the mid-19th century America was divided. The northern states had abolished slavery long ago, and in the southern states white farmers depended on slave labour and considered slaves their "property".

Abraham Lincoln

In 1860 Abraham Lincoln, who'd spoken out against the spread of slavery, was elected US president. This worried the southern states and they decided to try and go it alone and form a separate government. The North did not want the southern states to separate and in April 1861 a **civil war** erupted.

Frederick Douglass was determined to focus the American people on what they were really fighting for – freedom from slavery. He wrote lots of articles and travelled up and down the North, giving speeches and arguing against slavery.

Frederick at an anti-slavery rally in New York in the 1850s

The American Civil War: the northern states against the southern states at the start of the war

the northern states that wanted to end slavery all over the USA, and stay as one whole country

states that wanted to keep slavery but didn't want to join the southern states as a separate country

the southern states that wanted to become separate from the rest of the USA so they could keep slavery in the South

The Freedom Law

On New Year's Day 1863, a new law called the Freedom Law was passed to free all slaves in the southern states and all those who'd fled from the South. The law did not put an end to all slavery in America, though. It continued to exist in some states on the border between the South and the North. But it was a huge step forward, and Frederick wept with joy.

Frederick had been campaigning for black people to be allowed to fight for the North, and after this law was passed the northern army finally began to accept black men, though they were paid less and were not as well equipped as the white soldiers.

a regiment of black soldiers in 1863

More than 186,000 black soldiers signed up and formed into **regiments**. The most famous of these was the heroic Fifty-Fourth Massachusetts Regiment. Frederick himself recruited many of its men and his own sons, Lewis and Charles, were among the first to **enlist**.

the Fifty-Fourth Regiment in action during the Civil War

43

The end of the war

By the end of 1864 the North was winning the war and victory
finally came when, during very cold winter weather,
their armies marched down into the South. The soldiers of
the South were hungry and desperate and they fled, putting
an end to the war. It was about time, for over those last four years
600,000 men and boys had died fighting.

However, on 14th April 1865, a week after the Civil War finally ended, President Lincoln was shot and killed by a man who had supported the South. Frederick was devastated by the news – he felt Lincoln was a great leader. Later Lincoln's widow gave away her husband's old possessions to special friends and supporters. She gave Lincoln's favourite walking-stick to Frederick.

President Lincoln's funeral was attended by thousands of people.

45

Aftermath: fighting for the black vote

At the end of 1865, slavery was officially abolished throughout the United States. But black people still didn't have the same rights as whites and the southern states quickly passed new laws to limit the freedom of former slaves. These "Black Code" laws meant that black people were forbidden from buying land or holding certain jobs. Many ex-slaves lived in desperate conditions and were not much better off than when they had been slaves.

Black people often returned to live in the same poor homes they had lived in as slaves.

Also, black people didn't have the vote, which Frederick was now fighting hard for. "Slavery," he wrote, "is not abolished until the black man has the **ballot**."

Finally, in 1870, black men in the United States got the vote. This led to the first generation of black American politicians, but their power remained very limited.

Hiram Rhodes Revels was the first black man in government, in 1870

47

The Freedman's Bank

In 1872 Frederick and Anna's house in Rochester was burnt down by **arsonists**. They moved to Washington where Frederick was offered a job with the Freedman's Savings and Trust Company, a bank that had been specially set up to encourage black people to invest and save their money. Frederick was delighted when the company asked him to take over as president, but in 1874 the bank went bust and thousands of black Americans, including Frederick, lost their savings.

A few years later Frederick went to Maryland to revisit friends and family. He had left Maryland so many years ago and now wanted to go back and revisit his past. He called on his old slave-master Thomas Auld, who was now a weak, elderly man. Auld wept when he saw his former slave and told Frederick that he'd always known he was too clever to be a slave and that he'd followed news of his career for years. Frederick said he understood why Thomas had acted as he had and the men parted on good terms.

The end

In 1882 Anna died after she had a **stroke**. But grief did not slow
Frederick down and he continued to travel and give talks where
he spoke out against the desperate conditions of poor black farm
workers in the South. He also worked as a presidential adviser
and held a series of official posts including that of US representative
in the Caribbean island of Haiti. No black man had ever reached
such a senior position in the American government.

Frederick died of a heart attack in 1895, at the age of 77 and thousands of people visited the church where his coffin lay.

Frederick Douglass had fought nearly all his life for his own freedom and for the freedom of millions of black slaves. He is still remembered today as America's first great civil rights leader.

statue of Frederick Douglass in Harlem, New York

Glossary

abolitionist a person who wanted to put an end to slavery

arsonists people who burn down other people's buildings out of spite

ballot an election where people vote for their political leader

civil war a war between two groups of people in the same country

disobedience not doing what you're told

enlist join the army and become a soldier

executed to be killed by law as a punishment

fluent able to speak clearly and effectively, without hesitating

forged made a fake of something to trick people into thinking it is real

labourers people who do hard physical work

negro a word that was used to describe black people, which is now considered disrespectful and unacceptable

prejudice thinking bad things about someone for no good reason

regiments the groups that soldiers are organised into

spirit a person's strong feeling of who they are and what they want to do

stroke a sudden severe illness of the brain

Index

From slavery to freedom

born in Maryland, owned by Captain Aaron Anthony

hired to a kinder farmer, working shorter hours and set up a Sunday school for slaves

gave first speech for the American Anti-Slavery Society

published autobiography

1810s   1820s   1830s   1840s   1850

mother died; worked for the Auld family in Baltimore

worked for "slave-breaker" Edward Covey

toured Britain, giving talks

ran away to New York; married Anna Murray; settled in New Bedford, Massachusetts

returned to USA as a free man; settled in Rochester

American Civil War

became president of Freedman's Bank but the bank goes out of business soon after

Abraham Lincoln killed; slavery outlawed in the United States

died in Washington DC

1860s   1870s   1880s   1890s

black men in the United States got the vote

became US minister for Haiti

Freedom Law was passed

Ideas for reading

Written by Clare Dowdall BA(Ed), MA(Ed)
Lecturer and Primary Literacy Consultant

Learning objectives: make notes on and use evidence from across a text to explain ideas and events; identify how information texts are structured; explore how writers use language for dramatic effects; present a spoken argument, sequencing points logically, defending views with evidence and making use of persuasive language

Curriculum links: Citizenship; History

Interest words: abolitionist, ballot, civil war, disobedience, enlist, executed, fluent, forged, labourers, prejudice, regiments, spirit, stroke

Resources: whiteboard, internet, ICT

Getting started

This book can be read over two or more reading sessions.

- Look closely at the image of Frederick Douglass on the front cover. Ask children what they know about slavery, and whether Frederick looks as they imagine a slave would have looked. Discuss his appearance, and list adjectives on the whiteboard to describe him, e.g. proud, stern.

- Read the blurb. Discuss what the term "America's first great civil rights leader" might mean.

- Ask children to suggest what a biography is. Look at the contents together and notice how this biography is organized. Discuss whether a biography is a purely factual account, or may contain elements of author opinion.

Reading and responding

- Ask for a volunteer to read pp2–5 aloud to the group. Model how to collect and share as many facts as possible about Frederick's early childhood in order to provide a context to base further reading on.

- Discuss the language features of this biography. Help children to notice that it is written in the third person and in the past tense. Based on their reading, ask children to find examples of how the author has used language for dramatic effect, e.g. the description of plantations on p7. Discuss whether this account is purely factual, or whether there may be an element of author opinion.